This journal belongs to

....

Contact info

....

....

....

Date

....

Introduction

Writing takes practice and imagination. Whether you are writing a short story or a poem, fiction or essays, keeping it interesting means employing something that sparks curiosity, hooks the reader, or opens their eyes to new possibilities.

This journal is full of prompts that allow writers to practice imaginative writing. It asks you to think, describe, change point of view, reach, explain, focus, and dream. With every prompt, you exercise writing in new and different ways.

Dive in. Go in order or skip around. Just write as often as you can. Practice makes perfect and this journal is the perfect place to practice. And when you have a plot twist you would like to share, post it on Instagram or Facebook with the hashtag #MyPlotTwist and TAG @ellieclairegifts.

Happy writing!

Dreams make for good story prompts. Write a story
that incorporates a dream you've recently had.

....
....
....
....
....
....
....
....
....
....
....
....
....
....
....
....
....
....
....
....
....
....
....
....
....
....

Think about a word you rarely say or hear
(ie. woolgathering, quixotic, or thingamajig).
Write a poem/scene making use of that word.

....
....
....
....
....
....
....
....
....
....
....
....
....
....
....
....
....
....
....
....
....
....
....
....
....
....
....
....
....

Who is your hero? Describe him or her in a way that will make others feel the hero vibes like you do.

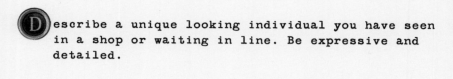

escribe a unique looking individual you have seen
in a shop or waiting in line. Be expressive and
detailed.

Have you ever seen a closed door and wondered what is behind it? Write a story about what's there and why it is important to keep the door closed or to get it opened.

....
....
....
....
....
....
....
....
....
....
....
....
....
....
....
....
....
....
....
....
....
....
....
....

If you followed a rainbow and found your greatest
desire at the end of it, what would that be?

....
....
....
....
....
....
....
....
....
....
....
....
....
....
....
....
....
....
....
....
....
....
....
....
....

Sit somewhere and listen for half an hour or longer. Write about what you hear: nature sounds, conversations, traffic.

....
....
....
....
....
....
....
....
....
....
....
....
....
....
....
....
....
....
....
....
....
....
....
....
....
....
....
....
....
....
....
....

Take pieces of your favorite sayings, phrases, or poems and fashion a new poem from them.

Describe your first bite or drink of something new, good or bad, including the taste, texture, temperature, reaction, place, and circumstances that led to you trying it.

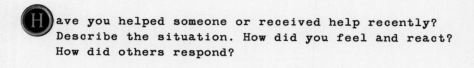

Have you helped someone or received help recently? Describe the situation. How did you feel and react? How did others respond?

....
....
....
....
....
....
....
....
....
....
....
....
....
....
....
....
....
....
....
....
....
....
....

Open your phone, computer, or a photo album. Write
a story or journal entry about the fifth photo
you find.

Visualization is vital to good storytelling. Write about someone by describing his or her clothing, hair, shoes, and/or makeup.

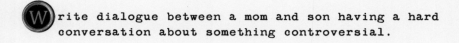

Write dialogue between a mom and son having a hard conversation about something controversial.

Stories usually involve some sort conflict, problem, or startling event. Write a scene or passage about two people in conflict and how they find resolution.

Listen to dialogue at work, a store, or in a movie. Using a few lines of it, take the dialogue in a new direction, add depth, or change the tone.

Write a character sketch of someone who has a serious character flaw including how they deal with the flaw and/or how they are treated because of it.

Write a character sketch of someone by describing only their emotional hot buttons or internal struggles and how that affects their outward actions.

Write about your favorite month of the year.

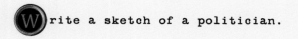

Write a sketch of a politician.

Describe a composite person, using characteristics from no fewer than three people you observe in your favorite café, coffee shop, or workout facility.

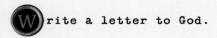**W**rite a letter to God.

Write dialogue between an older couple trying to understand why young people do what they do.

Write a letter to someone of significance.

Write about a state or country you've never been to.

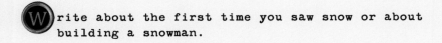

Write about the first time you saw snow or about building a snowman.

....
....
....
....
....
....
....
....
....
....
....
....
....
....
....
....
....
....
....
....
....
....
....
....
....

Write about a ship, train, or other vehicle that can take you somewhere far away from where you are now. Describe how it looks, how it moves, or how it makes you feel.

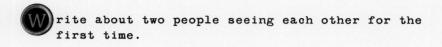

Write about two people seeing each other for the first time.

Open a dictionary, close your eyes, and point to the page. Use the word under your finger as the foundation for a story.

If your favorite beverage was outlawed, what would you do to get it? How you would smuggle the beverage in to your home, work, or country?

Think about the strangest thing you have seen in public—behavior, clothing, hairstyle, etc. Write a story or poem putting that strangeness in the middle of a normal, everyday scene.

....
....
....
....
....
....
....
....
....
....
....
....
....
....
....
....
....
....
....
....
....
....
....
....
....
....

Describe the moment, thought, or decision that turns someone from feeling worthless and irrelevant to fighting back into confidence and strength.

....

....

....

....

....

....

....

....

....

....

....

....

....

....

....

....

....

....

....

....

....

....

....

....

....

....

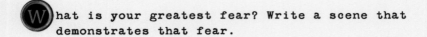

What is your greatest fear? Write a scene that
demonstrates that fear.

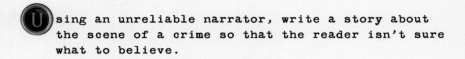

Using an unreliable narrator, write a story about the scene of a crime so that the reader isn't sure what to believe.

Using only text messages, write a love story.

I

magine you just discovered that the president is
an imposter. Write a plan of action for letting
the right people know without getting caught by
the people who put the imposter in power.

....
....
....
....
....
....
....
....
....
....
....
....
....
....
....
....
....
....
....
....
....
....
....

Describe the ocean as if the reader has never seen, smelled, or touched it before.

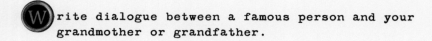

Write dialogue between a famous person and your grandmother or grandfather.

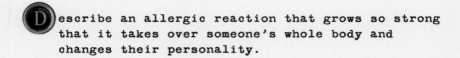

Describe an allergic reaction that grows so strong that it takes over someone's whole body and changes their personality.

Develop a character who is looking for world domination. Describe the kinds of people he/she would want on his/her side. What kind of characteristics would he/she need to be successful?

....
....
....
....
....
....
....
....
....
....
....
....
....
....
....
....
....
....
....
....
....
....
....
....
....
....
....
....
....

What characteristics do you feel make for an excellent leader? Write a character sketch about someone who has all of these qualities. Or write a sketch about a leader with none of them.

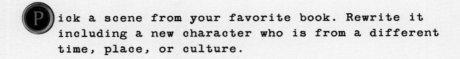
Pick a scene from your favorite book. Rewrite it
including a new character who is from a different
time, place, or culture.

....

....

....

....

....

....

....

....

....

....

....

....

....

....

....

....

....

....

....

....

....

....

....

....

....

....

....

....

....

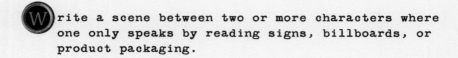

Write a scene between two or more characters where one only speaks by reading signs, billboards, or product packaging.

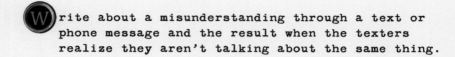

Write about a misunderstanding through a text or phone message and the result when the texters realize they aren't talking about the same thing.

....
....
....
....
....
....
....
....
....
....
....
....
....
....
....
....
....
....
....
....
....
....
....
....

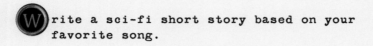

Write a sci-fi short story based on your favorite song.

....

....

....

....

....

....

....

....

....

....

....

....

....

....

....

....

....

....

....

....

....

....

....

....

....

....

....

....

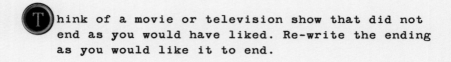

Think of a movie or television show that did not end as you would have liked. Re-write the ending as you would like it to end.

....
....
....
....
....
....
....
....
....
....
....
....
....
....
....
....
....
....
....
....
....
....
....
....
....
....
....
....
....
....
....

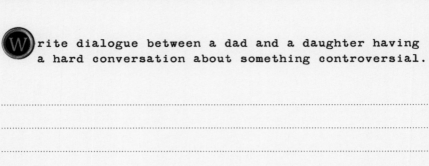

Write dialogue between a dad and a daughter having a hard conversation about something controversial.

Describe a wreck. Give details of direction, speed, location, sights, sounds, and smells.

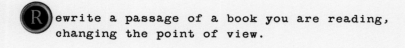

Rewrite a passage of a book you are reading, changing the point of view.

....
....
....
....
....
....
....
....
....
....
....
....
....
....
....
....
....
....
....
....
....
....
....
....
....
....
....
....
....
....
....
....
....
....

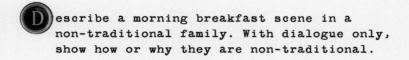

Describe a morning breakfast scene in a
non-traditional family. With dialogue only,
show how or why they are non-traditional.

An animal starts talking to a group of people. What does it say? How do the people react?

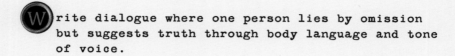

Write dialogue where one person lies by omission but suggests truth through body language and tone of voice.

Write a scene/story including some words from a language that is not your native language. Explain the unfamiliar words without giving the definition.

....

....

....

....

....

....

....

....

....

....

....

....

....

....

....

....

....

....

....

....

....

....

....

....

Describe a sunset so a blind person can "see" it.

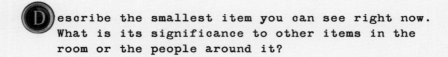

Describe the smallest item you can see right now. What is its significance to other items in the room or the people around it?

....

....

....

....

....

....

....

....

....

....

....

....

....

....

....

....

....

....

....

....

....

....

....

....

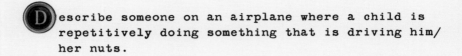
Describe someone on an airplane where a child is repetitively doing something that is driving him/her nuts.

Describe someone who is feeling pure, unadulterated joy. What does that look like to that person? What does it look like to someone witnessing that person's feelings?

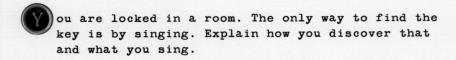

You are locked in a room. The only way to find the key is by singing. Explain how you discover that and what you sing.

Write about a song without using lines from the song.

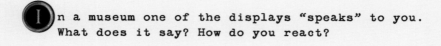

In a museum one of the displays "speaks" to you. What does it say? How do you react?

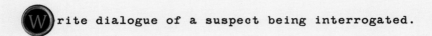

Write dialogue of a suspect being interrogated.

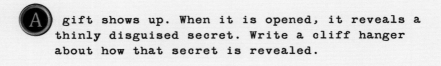

A gift shows up. When it is opened, it reveals a thinly disguised secret. Write a cliff hanger about how that secret is revealed.

....
....
....
....
....
....
....
....
....
....
....
....
....
....
....
....
....
....
....
....
....
....
....
....

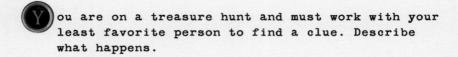
You are on a treasure hunt and must work with your least favorite person to find a clue. Describe what happens.

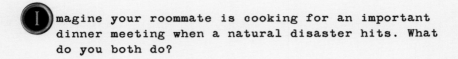

Imagine your roommate is cooking for an important dinner meeting when a natural disaster hits. What do you both do?

....
....
....
....
....
....
....
....
....
....
....
....
....
....
....
....
....
....
....
....
....
....
....
....
....
....
....
....
....
....
....
....
....
....
....
....
....
....

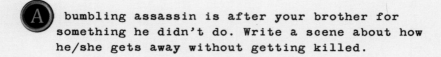

A bumbling assassin is after your brother for something he didn't do. Write a scene about how he/she gets away without getting killed.

....
....
....
....
....
....
....
....
....
....
....
....
....
....
....
....
....
....
....
....
....
....
....
....
....
....
....

Your best friend texts you to say she/he needs to use the restroom but is stuck in the office supply closet while the boss and his secretary are busy just outside the door. Write a text conversation that describes what happens next.

....
....
....
....
....
....
....
....
....
....
....
....
....
....
....
....
....
....
....
....
....
....
....

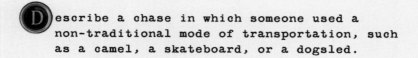

Describe a chase in which someone used a
non-traditional mode of transportation, such
as a camel, a skateboard, or a dogsled.

On the way to the grocery store, you get caught up in a funeral procession where you learn things about the deceased that bring events in your own life into clearer focus.

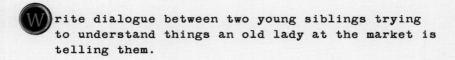

Write dialogue between two young siblings trying to understand things an old lady at the market is telling them.

Imagine witnessing a burglary and later encountering the burglar at your child's nursery.

Write a scene where someone leaves a coffee shop but picks up the wrong briefcase. The contents inside are unusual medical documents. Describe what happens when she/he reads them.

Write a dialogue between someone who has information that can stop an execution and the warden who does not want the execution stopped.

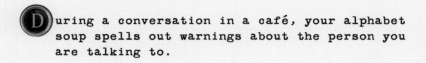

During a conversation in a café, your alphabet soup spells out warnings about the person you are talking to.

Write about someone whose family identity is shaken when he/she unearths an ancient book from the attic.

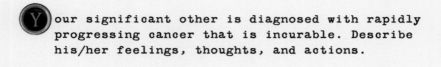

Your significant other is diagnosed with rapidly progressing cancer that is incurable. Describe his/her feelings, thoughts, and actions.

Write about someone falling through ice, trees, time, or some dimension in a very unexpected way.

Write dialogue where someone is having a conversation with him/herself.

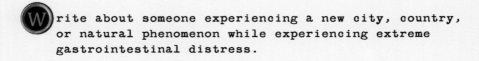

Write about someone experiencing a new city, country, or natural phenomenon while experiencing extreme gastrointestinal distress.

Describe someone who is addicted to something not usually associated with addiction like drawing, counting the hairs on her/his head, touching window latches. Demonstrate the addiction in a scene where it can't be ignored.

....
....
....
....
....
....
....
....
....
....
....
....
....
....
....
....
....
....
....
....
....
....
....
....
....
....
....
....
....
....

Ellie Claire
Hachette Book Group
1290 Avenue of the Americas, New York, NY 10104
ellieclaire.com

First edition: July 2020 (hardcover)

Ellie Claire is a division of Hachette Book Group, Inc. The Ellie Claire name and
logo are trademarks of Hachette Book Group, Inc.

Editorial direction by Marilyn Jansen

Print book interior design by Bart Dawson.

ISBN: 9781546014836

Printed in China
RRD-S
10 9 8 7 6 5 4 3 2 1